WE THE WILD SEAS

is a book of STORIES and POEMS and ART describing true voyages across and beyond the wild western waves and the secret seas of deep sleep, featuring epic tales:
DOLPHINS KEEP ME SAFE IN DREAMS
and
THE RUDDY USELESS FISHERMAN
and
THE SHIPWRECKED SAILOR.
and
various poems and stories
describing the author's long friendship with the sea.

Written and drawn by
Ed Boxall
Published by The Pearbox Press, 2025.
50 Edmund Road,
Hastings,
TN35 5LF
Text and images © Ed Boxall 2025
EDBOXALL.CO.UK

We the Wild Seas

Ed Boxall

Contents

We the Wild Seas	6
Reading the Dawn Treader	8
Dolphins Keep Me Safe in Dreams	10
Bunk Beds	44
Holes	46
Thinkthing	48
Mrs Gregg Goes Swimming	49
These Days Things Have Names	50
The Ruddy Useless Fisherman	54
Rock-a-Nore Baby	80
My First Jack in the Green	85
The Gods of Green Summer Awake	87
To the Gods of Green Summer	88
No Trains Home	90
Let's Get Fish and Chips	92
The Shipwrecked Sailor	94
The Island of Forgotten War	128

We the Wild Seas

We the waves of all wild seas
waves of every deep
whisper on forever from
all the galaxies

hear us in the passing cars
hear us in the breeze
sighing seas forever breathe
soothing you to sleep

let your mind get shipwrecked
let all intentions rest
let your thoughts be lost across
distant dark sea beds

fall to open pathless ways
in our endless deeps
our sighing songs murmur on
soothing you to sleep

we are all around and everywhere
in every breath you breathe
sleep in sighs of our soft song
surrender to sleep

Reading The Dawn Treader

Last night, as I read
The Voyage of the Dawn Treader
to my eight-year-old son,
he held light in his face
like branches hold sunlight on
motionless spring evenings.

It is the light from the last sea at the end of the world,
where on an island of soft low hills
a hermit sang an impossible song.

Together, we tried to hear.

Today he has been shouting GO AWAY
and has left a storm of banging doors behind him.

At bedtime tonight I sat on the end of his bed
and words sailed from my mouth
but got lost on their
rambling rudderless
quest for wisdom.

He replied with a short sharp squark.

But a little while later
he crept downstairs and pretended he was sick,
and as I put him back to bed,
his penguin waved.

I know we will be all right
because we have sailed together
on a bright dragon ship
called The Dawn Treader

and shared the still, silent light
at the end of the world.

Dolphins Keep Me Safe in Dreams

At bedtime I am terrified,
Of the moment I am left alone,
For I hear gossiping in the dark,
And from my pillow ghostly goblins groan.

The deathly sound of voices grows,
I whisper to the tuneless drone,
"I don't like you, go away,
Leave my pillow, leave my home"

From far oceans, dolphins hear,

They nose between my clenching toes,

They dive across the duvet waves,

And chase away the pillow ghosts.

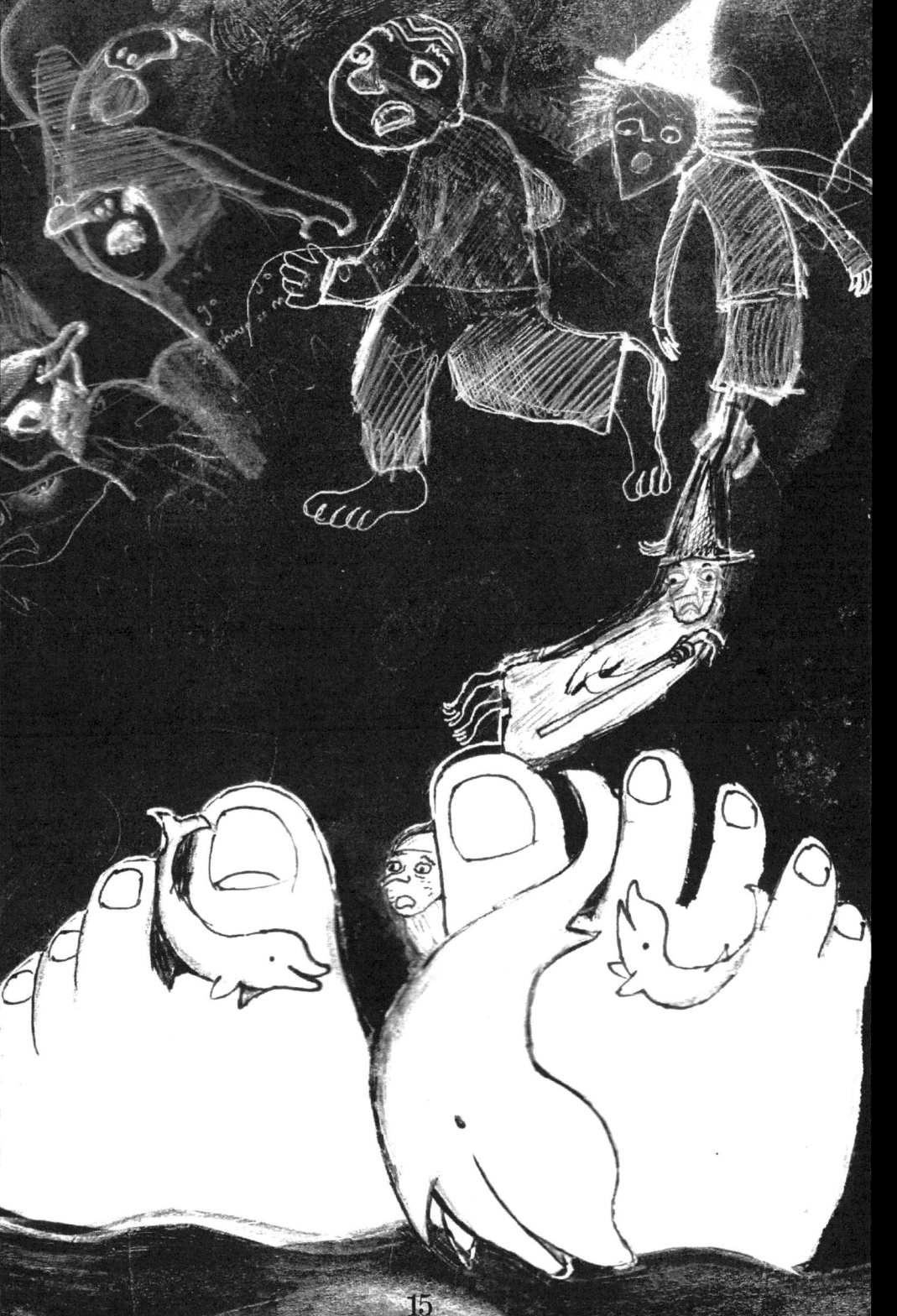

My bed becomes a barrel boat,

Waves beneath me fall and rise,

Dolphins dive and dance and play

As we sail away on the shimmering tide.

Far from cars and clocks and phones,

Drifting ocean days are long,

We sail so far we hear the stars,

Like a friendly murmur of radio song.

I find my long departed grandad,
On the garden isle of Dinkerdire,

I hear his warm familiar voice,
From my cosy place by the bright campfire.

Unicorns live in a ruined fort,

On the forest island of Toonaneen,

They sing me secrets of forgotten times, I only remember in my deepest dreams.

We sail to the junk yard isle of Dritch,

Where I lost my sock in a forest of doors,

To nameless nowheres not yet begun,
Where no one has ever been before.

Further still to a silent sea,

Where the pillow ghosts are trapped in stone,

Misty statues, harmless now,

We pass on quickly and head for home.

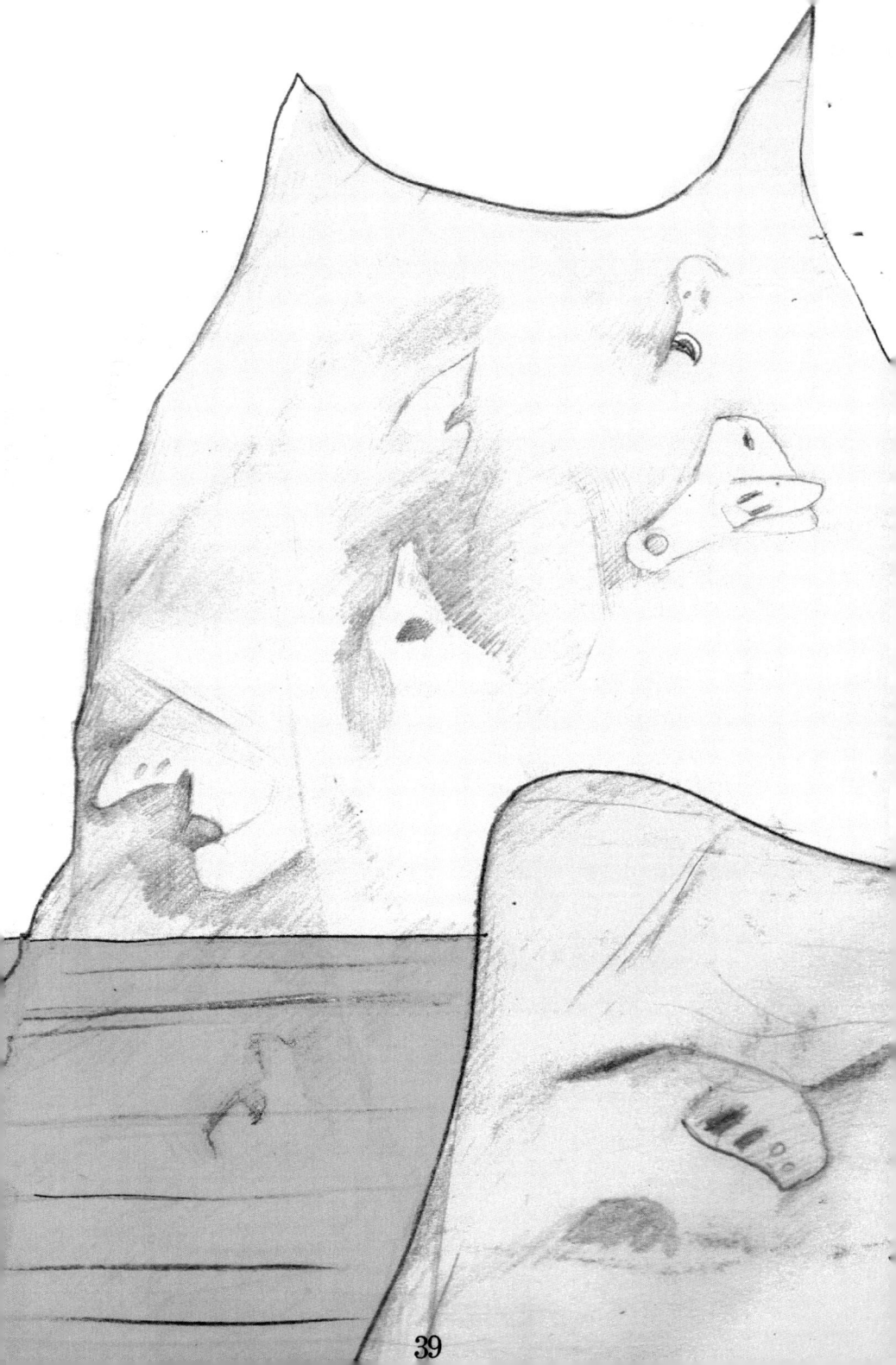

Every night I sail away,
To islands on my secret sea,
Faraway and home by dawn,
Dolphins keep me safe in dreams.

Bunk Beds

When we visit Nanna and Grandad my big brother
gets the top bunk of course.
But bottom bunk is best for me
because it's my cabin on my yellow submarine.

I have everything I need for the journey-
a tiny mother of pearl pen knife,
a small notebook with a glossy colourful picture of a
steam train on the cover,
and my toy Paddington.

And best of all, the wooden box
Grandad made with me today.
It still smells of fresh pine
and is perfectly smooth from
rubbing with fine sandpaper.

There is plenty of space for all my things,
even though Grandad has already put in
a universe of kindness.

On my undersea journey
my torchlight finds a bright pink cake castle
on the back page of the Beano annual that lives on the
bookshelf at the bottom of the bed.

My torchlight finds the barnacled underbellys of
plesiosaurs and megadons swiftly passing above.

And my torchlight finds 52 year old me,
writing this at my kitchen table,
the box I made with Grandad that day,
beside me.

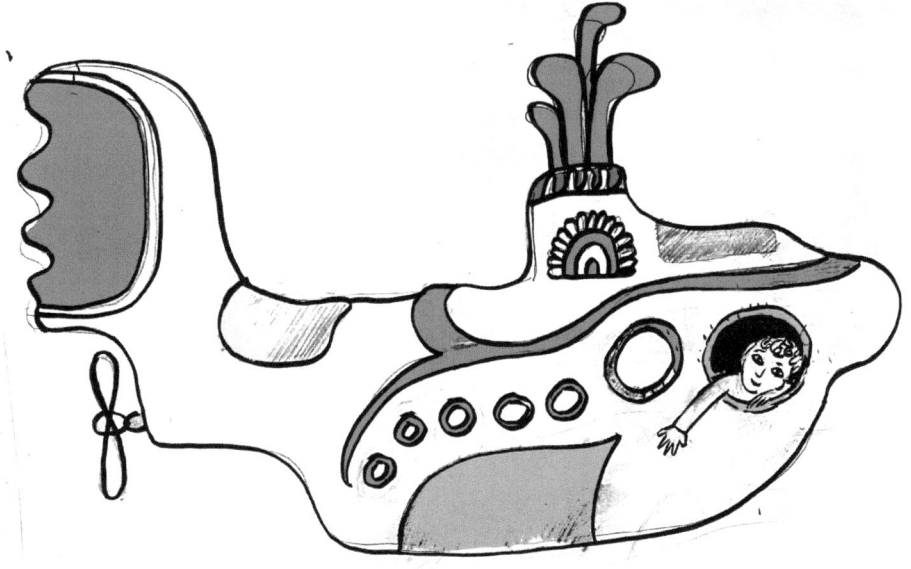

Holes

I wonder why my brother and I always preferred digging deep holes on the beach to building sandcastles. Sandcastle building was a more common and traditional practice among children in the late 1970s. But we would dig holes in the golden sand of Lowestoft beach with wild enthusiasm and serious commitment. I don't remember ever building a sandcastle.

There were two aims to beach hole digging:
1. To dig a really deep hole
2. To find water.

Now, there was an awful lot of water in easy reach. A whole North Sea of it. You really didn't *need* to dig to find water. But we dug to discover a sea for ourselves. We dug to find our own small sea. We were making our myth of the sea with spades and sand and buckets.

The moment we found water, perhaps 3 feet down, was always exciting. We'd dig deeper, and a tiny puddle would quickly become a pond.

At that point, our heroic achievement could be rewarded. We gave ourselves permission to build a river to the sea so we could harvest water from that abundant supply a few feet away. We could feed our little sea from the great cosmic mystery of the North Sea. And now the river banks and beaches of the land we had made could be decorated with hills, shells, towers, bridges, dead crabs, seaweed and pebbles. A civilisation could be built.

Today, I am continuing to dig that big hole with different tools. Today, I am writing my myth of the sea with pens, pencils, printing ink, my iPad and laptop. I am feeding my little sea from the water of Big Time Sea.

thinkthing

thinkthing
is a swimthing
a sort of brightshadow springing thing

sleek
winged spinthing

escaping

to the wide open
seathing

Mrs Gregg Goes Swimming

At lunchtime today,
instead of microwaving her soup,
and eating at her usual table in the staff room,
Mrs Gregg parked around
the corner from school,
and cried.

You see, her dad has an illness
that makes him a stranger,
and it's hard for her to think of anything
but his face full of questions
that he cannot ask,
and she can never answer.

So, Mrs Gregg was late back to playground duty
which meant year 5 and 6
had to wait 10 minutes to go outside.

After school today,
Mrs Gregg drove to the beach.
She wrapped herself in a big old towel
covered in a smiling sunshine face design,
and awkwardly changed into
her swimming costume underneath.

Then, without hesitating for a moment,
she dived into the sea.

    sudden cold brilliance
   pushed all thoughts away
she darted free from
     the heavy hard net of day
     her tears swam away
   with sparkling shoals
 of tiny fish
she surfaced as
    a wild wordless
      curious thing
     of tingling skin
   playing with
arms legs fingers toes wiggling stretching
        and splashing
          away the day

Mrs Gregg was suddenly unsure of how much time
she had been in the water.
So, she swam back to shore.
As she swam she was careful
to keep her fingers closed and to spread her arms right out
like her dad taught her, a long time ago.

After her swim,
Mrs Gregg sat on her towel,
and worried about how
year 5 and 6 lost
10 minutes of their playtime
because she was late back
to playground duty
earlier that day.

These Days Things have Names.

These days things have names.

For example:

Sea
Beach
Pebble
Bird

Names are recent ripples
on the surface of Big Time Sea.

The Ruddy Useless Fisherman

The Town

The town was called Felldun. Felldun was a little town by the sea, with cobbled streets and cottages, fish and chip shops, pubs and cafes. And there was a shop called the 'The Mermaid's Hat' that sold buckets, spades, dream-catchers, fossils, crystals, batteries and sun lotion. And books of local stories by local writers, like this one. Perhaps you're standing in the Mermaid's Hat right now reading this. Go on- buy this book! The rest of the story is fabulous, I promise.

There were a few small fishing boats in the small fishing harbour. And a few fishermen. Two of whom were Rufus and Dan. The heroes of this story.

Rufus

Rufus was a ruddy useless fisherman.

He spent far too much time making up imaginary lives for lobsters, and often caught himself and let the fish go.

He once tugged the wangle winch the wrong way because he was talking to himself about squirrels. And, once, he sewed himself inside the net when he was mending it.

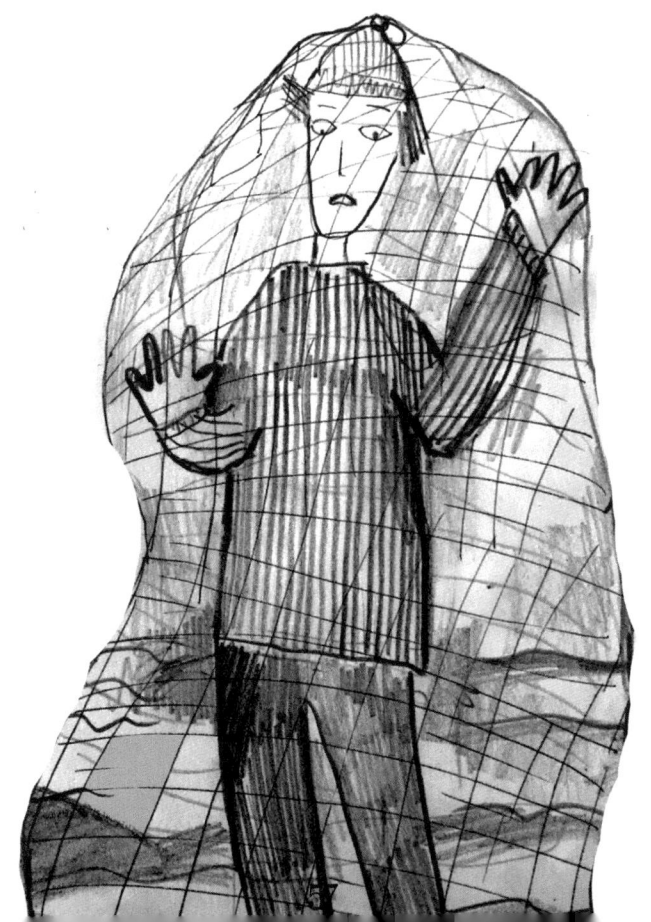

Dan

Dan, who was Rufus' boss, mumbled 'ruddy useless fisherman' under his breath when Rufus messed up. He said it a lot. Dan was a ruddy good fisherman.

He was old and had been fishing for many years. He was as solid, silent and tough as the biggest rocks on the beach. Talking to him was a bit like talking to those rocks. He listened, but he didn't say much. He was always certain he knew best and he was usually right.

Dan was a softy inside though. In fact his favourite thing about fishing was getting away from shore and playing romantic songs he remembered from his childhood really loud. He'd sing along at the top of his voice as he worked, often with tears in his eyes.

Rufus never laughed at Dan doing this like the other fishermen did. Rufus and Dan were friends.

The Giant

Faraway from Felldun a giant looked out over the top of the forest where he lived.

The giant, who was just a small child (well, a massive, giant small child) was full of wild, restless energy and in the mood to play.

A Crew of Two

Dan's boat was called 'Agnetha'. It had a small crew. A crew of two. Dan and Rufus. Everyone else refused to work with Rufus. This story begins on an April morning when Dan and Rufus were getting ready for a fishing trip.

Rufus was determined to be a ruddy *good* fisherman on the trip. He knew that Dan would give up hope on him ever being good if he didn't get better at fishing soon.

Rufus had done everything right on the beach. He'd packed the tools in the right place, helped with the grindle cropper without disaster and had got the food ready for the trip. As always Dan had said

"I'll eat anything just not ruddy fish"

They left harbour and by the time the sun was high in the sky the shore was out of sight. It was a beautiful Spring day.

The Ruddy just-about-okay Fisherman

Rufus had tried so hard all day, and by evening a couple of boxes were full of fish.

Not a bad start.

Dan was starting to think Rufus would be a fisherman after all.

He hummed happily to himself as they sorted the fish. Dan saw Rufus yawning and said he could go for a break.

This was when it happened.

It happened as it always did.

It happened as the bright day faded into soft grey of evening and the sky glowed orange and yellow and gold.

It Happens

Rufus looked down over the edge of the boat.

He felt his mind drift with the lapping of the waves.

The evening breeze moved across the water and the sea disappeared.

Instead he saw the shadows of the clouds scamper over mountain peaks below him.

To Rufus, they were flying. Not sailing.

He saw barren rocky ground scattered with colossal boulders. He saw the reflection of the bottom of the boat glide over perfectly still, deep blue mountain lakes. The mountains disappeared below into mist, hiding the valleys below .

It was a more fresh and wild and outdoors than anywhere he had ever been.

A great eagle flew right up close to the boat, gliding underneath.

It had happened. Suddenly, Rufus was seeing the *other* world. The place he called 'The Land Between Tick and Tock'. A place Rufus *could* see, but Dan, and all other humans, could not.

The Land Between Tick and Tock

Rufus sung quietly to himself:

You hear the lapping of waves,
I hear the wind whistle
High over mountain tops,
In The Land Between Tick and Tock

You see the flat horizon,
I see the deep valley mist,
I long to get lost,
In The Land Between Tick and Tock

You go to sea to catch fish,
I seek the edge of our world,
and to look far beyond,
To The Land Between Tick and Tock

You find our world so easy,
I get everything wrong,
I'd like to start again
In The Land Between Tick and Tock.

While you live
a second in our world,
I live long lovely hours, flying high above,
The Land Between Tick and Tock.

After gazing at The Land Between Tick and Tock for what felt like hours, Rufus looked at the clock and saw that not a second had passed. He looked up. The mountains were gone and the sea had returned.

The Land Between Tick and Tock sent him into a daydream that turned him into that ruddy useless fisherman again. He messed up the winch mangles and mangled up the scrubbers. He slippped on the slimies and knocked a box of best cod into the sea.

However hard he tried Rufus' mind was on The Land Between Tick and Tock, not fishing. By nightfall Dan had given up on Rufus. The other fishermen were right, he thought, Rufus would never be a good fisherman.

The Forest

During the night, Rufus looked out over the sparkling moonlit sea, unable to sleep.

The night breeze moved across the water and the sea was gone.

This time they were flying over a forest in The Land Between Tick and Tock.

He saw the tops of huge trees looming out of the mist.

The trees were so huge it sometimes took an hour to pass over one tree.

The trunks disappeared below. The ground out of sight.

A breeze that tasted of impossible and faraway touched his lips,

And a silver humming bird fluttered by.

He wondered what it was like down there.

He longed to find out.

He felt like hours had passed, but he looked up at the moon of our world, and saw it hadn't moved. No time had passed.

The Giant

Rufus saw something moving in the distance in The Land Between Tick and Tock.

It was a figure. A person. A person who stood as tall as the trees and was looming out of the mist and heading straight towards Rufus.

A giant. A giant child. But still defintely a giant.

He had a wickedly playful look in his eyes. As the minutes passed Rufus saw the giant getting bigger and bigger and closer and closer as he walked towards them through the forests of the Land Between Tick and Tock.

Rufus shook Dan awake.

He begged Dan to take them home.

But getting Dan to listen was like getting the rocks on Felldun beach to change their mind.

They sailed towards the giant.
The giant strode towards them.

The Giant and The Toy Boat

If only, this once, Dan had listened to Rufus and changed his mind.

The worst storm Dan had ever known was upon them. The boat was like a tiny toy thrown by mountainous waves and the angry wind.

Dan saw the storm. Rufus saw the giant.

Rufus could see that to the giant the boat really was a toy. He threw it from hand to hand and way up into the sky, laughing thunderously at Dan and Rufus as they stumbled and slipped around the deck.

The giant threw them way up into the air, and just before the boat came crashing down into a treetop, Rufus leapt out boat and landed on the giant's shoulder. He looked down with horror to see that Dan lay motionless on the deck. He had been knocked out. Rufus had to face the giant alone.

The Giant Lullaby

The giant strode on towards the shore of Felldun. Rufus *had* to stop him reaching the town. He held tightly to one of the giants wiry hairs and begged him to stop. He kicked him in the ear and screamed. The giant didn't even notice.

With nothing left to try, Rufus started to sing. He sang the last song he had heard: 'Mammia Mia' by Abba. When he sang the giant slowed down. His eyes took on a faraway look as if he was thinking of something he missed.

Rufus sang every song he had heard Dan sing. And then songs from years ago and worlds away came to his lips. The songs became wordless and strange like a song of a silver humming bird.

Rufus sang, the giant slowed down. The giant stopped.

Rufus sang through sunsets, moon rises, the births and deaths of stars, through winds and snows and storms. He sang of hilly lands of long ago, he had forgotten he had known. It was a lonely tune of faraway, It was a cosy song of home that the giant also seemed to know. It would take a giant lullaby to send a giant child to sleep.

The Choice

At last the giant lay down in the mist and his eyes closed. Rufus felt he had been sleeping and had woken up. The song had been like a wonderful dream.

Rufus wanted to climb down the giant into the mist below. He longed to leave our world and see what he would find in The Land Between Tick and Tock.

But he knew he had to get Dan home. He crept away and climbed over to the tree where Agnetha was stuck.

He worked quickly breaking branches to free the boat. He found the deck of the boat covered in thousands of leaves that had fallen from the trees. He brushed them away to find Dan beneath, knocked out and fast asleep.

He started up the engine, and as the boat pulled away from the tree, Rufus watched the surface of the sea wash over the sleeping giant covering him like a great blanket.

Then The Land Between Tick and Tock was gone and the sea stretched to the horizon once more.

The Departure

When Rufus returned to shore he was greeted by a crowd who were as amazed as they were happy.

For, it turned out, the boat had been lost for a year and Dan and Rufus were presumed dead. But here was Dan, yawning and waking up with just a few bumps and bruises, feeling as if he'd been away for no more than a day. His eyes were wide as he looked around him at the deck.
Because those leaves from the tree from The Land Between Tick and Tock were now... fish

But Rufus no longer wanted to be a fisherman. With the money from the fishing trip he bought a tiny old sail boat.

Rufus sailed away forever in search of The Land Between Tick and Tock and the people of the town never saw him again.

But one fisherman really missed him.

Rock a Nore Baby

Rock-a-Nore is a rocky beach on the east side of Hastings. Blenny are a small fish, common in Rock-a-Nore rock pools.

One day, I was walking across the rocks on Rock a Nore Beach when I found a baby

She was sitting in a rockpool, trying to catch fish with her podgy little hands. She caught a blenny and put it in her mouth. The tail flapped for a moment before it went down her throat and a satisfied burp popped out.

I spent the long low tide hours finding her gifts from the tide line. She liked the bright novelty of land things: a plastic Pinocchio, orange string, a pink croc, a plastic brush with yellow bristles, a bleached white toothpaste tube, and a pair of broken sunglasses.

The afternoon slowly moved in the lilt of beach time. Low waves lapped among the rock pools, wind fell and rose and clouds hung perfectly still on the horizon as if they would never change. But every time I looked away and back again they spread new shapes against the blue sky.

Rock a Nore Baby sat in her pool, playing with her gifts.
Every time I looked away and back again she had changed too.
Her skin grew a little more shimmering and translucent. Her eyes grew a little larger, growing ready to see her way through the dark depths.

Soon the bright gifts I had given her floated on the rising water around her. Now she expertly kept afloat in the deep water with her webbed feet and steadying tail. The sun faded, the air softened and it was time for her to swim away. She gripped my arm with one of her tentacles, demanding I join her.

But I had to peel it off and let her go. I can't move between worlds like she can. But there are still faint red scars on my arms where Rock-a-Nore Baby gripped me.

Jack in the Green

Four poems in celebration of 'Jack in the Green',
the May Day celebrations that take place
every year in my seaside home town of Hastings:

My First Jack in the Green
The Gods of Green Summer are Alive
To the Gods of Green Summer
No Trains Home

My First Jack in the Green.

My May Day Bank Holiday trip to the seaside
felt like a bad idea as rain drizzled outside
the steamed-up windows of the café
where I tore open a little paper sachet
and poured sugar into my tea.

I craved my sofa and some easy TV
as I checked the train times home on my phone
and absentmindedly wiped
condensation from the window
and through the small patch of clear glass
a green goat horned face smiled back and

shouted *The Gods of Green Summer are Awake!*

The little goatmangod waved his mossy staff
and roared me away on thundering drums
to dance like a toddler with
glimmering smiles
                        bright eyes
        twisted horns
black beaks
    donkey heads
               hairy arms
      filthy nails
             fertile breathe
corsets   capes and
               coloured smoke

           gigantic antlers
                              bright rags
                                              rasping fiddles
                         wheezing accordions
                                              rumbling racking
                                              wacking drums

                         ...the Gods of Green Summer are awake!
                         ...the Gods of Green Summer are awake!

                              At dawn they had woken from
                              their deep slow churchstone sleep,
                                     and brushed earth
                              and dead leaves from their eyes,
                                   stretched, burped, farted
                              and stomped their way through
                                       the leafy shades of
                              The Old Paths to this town.

                                I joined them on their way
                              up the hill past the clapping crowds,
                         picnicking families and weekend drinkers,
                                 to the top of the West Hill.

                                           For May Day.

                                        For Jack in the Green.

The Gods of Green Summer are Awake

On this day the streets belong to
The Gods of Green Summer.

Today is their proud procession.

They have come alive for this fast-flickering season.

They call us mortals from cafes,
cars and carpeted rooms
to the wild adventure of Summer.

Now I am ready for ivy night rambles
I am ready for all-night raggle tangles
and thornyscratch scrambles.

I am ready for Summer to begin.

To the Gods of Green Summer

Gods of Green Summer I solemnly swear
to drink green sunshine with scarecrows
Gods of Green Summer I solemnly swear
to burn my list of things to do and bury my phone
Gods of Green Summer I solemnly swear
to eat cold custard from a broken mug in a rhododendron bush
Gods of Green Summer I solemnly swear
to leap from the witch's cauldron remade and reborn.
Gods of Green Summer I solemnly swear
to run along the harbour arm, dive into the sea,
and surface with a fish in my teeth.
Now I am ready for Summer.
And I see so clearly
how long, and wide, and deep it can be.

No Trains Home

The Gods of Green Summer
breathed a deep blanket of ivy over the railway station.
They tied roots around the train wheels,
sowed nettle thickets through the tracks,
and conjured rosy hot mesmeric air,
so the station staff
talk visionary gibberish
or sleep in the branches of the bright trees
that now burst through platform 4.

There will be no trains home.
This trip to the seaside
will last forever.

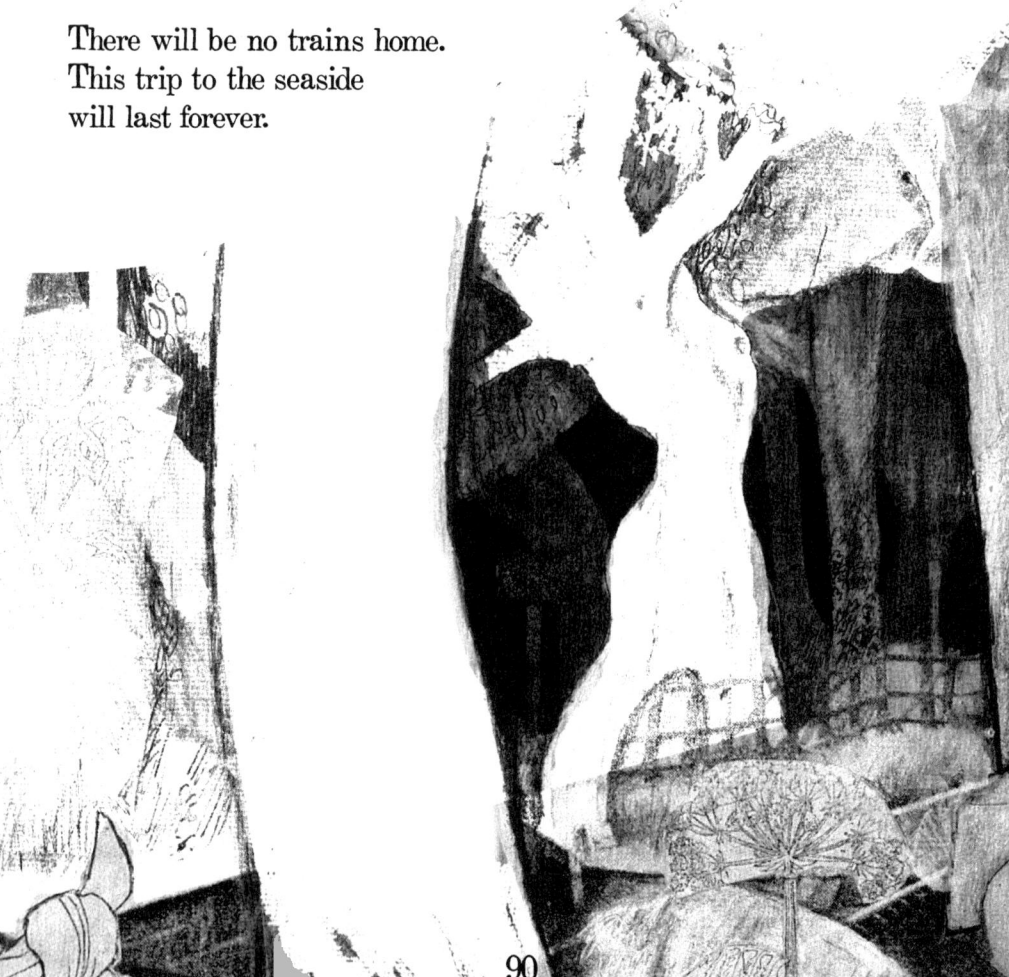

Fish and Chips

Let's get fish and chips tonight!
We deserve a treat.
Let's get fish and chips
after all, it's a day of the week.

Let's get fish and chips tonight
because today we did some stuff-
a bit of this and a bit of that
and a little slice of much.

Let's get fish and chips tonight
because we moved around and said words.
We deserve a reward
for (maybe) doing (a bit) better than our worst.

Let's get fish and chips tonight,
we really deserve that treat.
We got through the whole long day,
without losing our feet.

Let's get fish and chips tonight,
it's a day to celebrate
being here eating, and watching telly,
together, in the same place.

The Shipwrecked Sailor

I left the noise of the funfair,

And found a wild beach,

Where the only sounds
were the wind and waves,
And the seagull's lonely screech.

I met a shipwrecked sailor there,
Sitting on the rocks,
He introduced me to his crew:
A toucan and an old sheepdog.

I helped him mend his broken boat,

While he told me where they had been,

From wild countries behind the sky,

To the ocean's dark ravines.

By the time the moon was high,
The boat was as good as new,
I decided I would join them,
As I had nothing better to do.

We sailed a path of moonlight,
The shore soon out of sight,

To the enchanted misty place,
Where the horizon meets the sky.

We drifted to an island,

Where the air was warm and sweet,

I heard the voice of a lonely moon,
From the bottom of the sea,
Sing "We will have wild adventures,
If you come and live with me"

Her song pulled me on,
Like a moth towards lamplight,
I forgot my home, my name, my life,
I swam with all my might.

But the mermaid said 'don't listen',

Monsters chased me away,

The wise old sailor found me,

And kindly he explained,

"You must live in your own world,
There's so much you would miss,
Your toys, your books, your own room,
Your mother's bedtime kiss"

So I asked my friends to take me home,
Back along that sparkly path,
I was home in time for dinner,
A story and a bath.

Sometimes when the moon is full,
I wonder what would have been,
If I had stayed at sea that day,
And lived a life of dream.

Island of Forgotten War

One day all weapons of war will rot,
beneath the peaceful shores,
and the swaying grass, and deep soft moss,
of The Island of Forgotten War.

Among bright hills and valleys,
colossal trees will grow,
their roots will spread among the bones of war,
silenced forever below.

Fine networks of mycelium
will have grown through deep slow time,
to tangle the cold grey death machines,
with wondrous webs of life.

Peace will rest forevermore
on the island of old forgotten war.

Tourists will arrive in ferry boats,
for drifting worry free days,
safe and free as they chat and laugh,
in Sunny Shores Café .

Among the sand, children will collect,
sea smoothed scraps of war metal,
and drop them into colourful buckets,
with their spiral shells and pebbles.

Bright birds will glide up high,
children will roll down slopes,
couples will hike with backpacks and maps,
as summer sea winds blow.

Peace will rest forevermore
on the island of old forgotten war.

No one will really know,
how and why the island was made,
though there will be a small museum,
with some theories on display.

Some will think the final war-winners,
built it in celebration,
some will think it was sacred,
for a long forgotten religion.

The roar of war will be so long gone,
it will just be a weird old myth-
a cruel and silly childish thing,
we olden-time folk once did.

Peace will rest forevermore
on the island of old forgotten war.